Kindness
the Individual

An Introduction to

Vasily Grossman's

"Life and Fate"

David Conduct

For Russians, Ukrainians

and

Everyone Else

~This Book~

For Anna

With love from

Dave

X X X

Acknowledgements

Grateful acknowledgement is made to the following for permission to quote material in copyright:

- Vintage Press for excerpts from *Life and Fate*

- Pen and Sword Military for excerpts from *The Life and Fate of Vasily Grossman*

- Penguin for excerpt from *Day of Life and Death and Escape to the Moon*

Bibliography

Works by Vasily Grossman:

Life and Fate Vintage 2011

Everything Flows Vintage 2011

The Road MacLehose Press 2011

Works about Vasily Grossman:

J. and C. Garrard (2012) *The Life and Fate of Vasily Grossman.* Pen and Sword Military

A. Beevor (Ed.) (2005) *A Writer at War.* The Harvill Press

The Holy Bible

D. Conduct (2017) *The Holy Contour of Life.* Publish Nation

W.Saroyan (1971) *Days of Life and Death and Escape to the Moon.* Michael Joseph

INTRODUCTION

"Ah Bartleby! Ah humanity!"

Herman Melville

Bartleby the Scrivener

The present work is an attempt to distil the essence of Vasily Grossman's epic novel, *Life and Fate*, in the hope that this will encourage others to read the book. As Linda Grant observes in her introduction to the novel[1], weighing in at over 800 pages, *Life and Fate* can be a daunting, monumental read. I share her concern that this may deter readers from undertaking the task, for a book unread by many people is like the imprisoned version of *Life and Fate* that Grossman knew. We need to remember the events to which Vasily Grossman bears witness and I offer this text as a simple incentive to that end, and as a reminder of the importance of kindness in human affairs.

---

[1] Vasily Grossman (2011) *Life and Fate*. Vintage Press

THE ROAD FROM BERDICHEV

"Thou hast exposed us to the taunts

Of our neighbours, to the mockery

And contempt of all around.

Thou hast made us a byword

Among the nations and the

Peoples shake their heads at us."

Ps. 44 v 13, 14

Berdichev plays a pivotal role in the life of Vasily Grossman: the place of his birth and the place of his mother's murder by the Nazis. West of Kiev, in the Ukraine, the town of Berdichev had a population of around sixty thousand at the time of Grossman's birth. Of that number thirty thousand were Jews, making Berdichev a centre of Jewish religion and culture, referred to by Ukrainians as the 'Yids' capital'.

Though born of Jewish parents Grossman was never a practising Jew. In fact, he despised Berdichev and left it as soon as he could for studies in Kiev and Moscow. His parents came from the professional upper class and had no interest in Judaism or any other religion. They spoke and read Russian, not Yiddish. His mother was fluent in French and his father, who had studied engineering at Berne University in Switzerland, knew German very well. As such, they found themselves in the middle of two communities neither of which would accept them: the poor Jews of the 'shtetl', or ghetto, and the Christian Russian Orthodox community of the Ukraine who despised the Jews.[1]

Grossman's parents were born in the reign of the reforming Tsar Alexander II (1855 – 1881): his father, Semyon Osipovich, in 1870 and his mother

[1] Garrard, J & C. (2012) *The Life and Fate of Vasily Grossman* p.32

Yekaterina Savelievna, in 1871. Coming from the Jewish merchant class they both enjoyed a privileged status, particularly in the enlightened years of Tsar Alexander II's reign. His assassination in 1881, however led to a return to anti-Semitism under Alexander III and Nicholas II (1881 – 1917) and may have encouraged both of Grossman's parents to study at university in Switzerland where, in fact, they met and married.

Vasily Grossman was born in Berdichev on 12 December 1905 against a background of seething discontent in Russia, following the nation's humiliating defeat in war against Japan 1904 – 5 and the subsequent spontaneous revolution against Tsar Nicholas II's repressive and incompetent regime. Inevitably, these disturbances led to widespread persecution of the Jews, particularly in Grossman's native Ukraine.

At the age of five Grossman went with his mother to Switzerland where he lived until he was seven. In 1914 he entered the Kiev Modern High School. When Civil War broke out in Russia in 1918 he returned with his mother to Berdichev where he continued his studies and also worked in a lumber yard.

Some family crisis, coinciding with his mother's decision to take him to Switzerland seems to have caused Grossman's parents to split up and from 1910 he remained in his mother's care. The parents maintained an amicable correspondence but without any maintenance allowance on the part of Grossman's father. This obliged Grossman's mother to share a home in Berdichev with her sister and try to make money herself by tutoring French to private pupils. As a boy, therefore, Grossman, brought up by a devoted mother, Yekaterina, lived the life of a poor relation dependent on charity, and a Jew at odds with his Jewish identity.

Grossman's teenage years were very much overshadowed by the catastrophic events of Revolution and Civil War. He was twelve when the Bolshevik Revolution occurred and sixteen when the bloody Civil War came to an end. In this tumultuous period anti-Semitism was again prevalent and according to a Soviet estimate at least 150,000 Jews in the Ukraine were murdered in 1919 – 1920. On balance, the Bolsheviks seemed to support Jewish and other minority rights and this may explain Grossman's support for the revolutionary cause and the Bolshevik creation of a Soviet Union.

In 1921 Grossman enrolled on a preparatory course of the Kiev Higher Institute of National Education prior to embarking on a science degree course at Moscow University in 1923. Renewing contact with his father, a chemical engineer, at this point in his life gave Grossman a new found optimism in his future prospects as a scientist. And this was combined with faith in the capacity of the Bolshevik revolution to create a new country of the Soviet Union in which he, and all other Jews, would have equal rights as citizens.

The optimism with which Grossman began his university studies in 1923, however, was short-lived. His university career was a struggle financially and his father's maintenance support was barely sufficient. The problem was made worse in 1928 by his decision to get married which perhaps reflects his lack of commitment to his degree studies. Moreover, during his time at Moscow University he had discovered an unexpected talent as a writer. Encouraged by a cousin, Nadia, who was a party activist, Grossman began writing articles on social questions which attracted the attention of party journals such as 'Pravda' and also brought in some much needed cash.

Thus, after graduating in December 1929 and obtaining a job as a safety inspector in a mine in the industrial region of Donbass, Grossman continued with his literary interests and by the mid-1930's he was a well-established writer and a member of the prestigious Union of Soviet Writers.

Against the background of the Terror Famine 1930 – 32 in the Ukraine and the Moscow Treason Trials orchestrated by Stalin in the period 1935 – 37, however, Grossman's faith in the Bolshevik Revolution began to weaken. This growing disenchantment with the Stalinist regime was, of course, reinforced by Grossman's experience in the Second World War.

As a war correspondent with the Red Army in the Battle for Stalingrad he bore witness to Stalin's exploitation of the individual idealism and heroism of the Russian soldier and this was compounded by his experience of the 'Shoah', or Final Solution, as the Red Army advanced westward into the Ukraine and Poland. The discovery of the murder of his mother in Berdichev and Grossman's realisation of the enormity of Nazi and Stalinist evil were to provide the motivating force behind his novel, *Life and Fate*.

THE ROAD TO BERDICHEV AND BEYOND

"Because of thee we are done to death

All day long, and are treated as

Sheep for slaughter."

Ps. 44 v. 22.

"They have dug a pit before me."

Ps. 57 v. 6.

"How long shall the wicked, o Lord

How long shall the wicked exult?

They beat down thy people, o Lord,

And oppress thy chosen nation.

They murder the widow and the stranger

And do the fatherless to death."

Ps. 94 v. 3-6.

After the defeat of Nazi forces at Stalingrad, Vasily Grossman advanced with the Red Army westwards and by October 1943 he was in the Ukraine. Here he became more and more aware of his own Jewishness and more and more a witness of the Holocaust. He was among the first to record the massacre of Soviet Jewry in a report called *Ukraine without the Jews* (1943) which documented the German Persecution of all Jews in occupied Ukraine. 'All is silence. Everything is still. A whole people have been brutally murdered.'[2]

In part of this report Grossman simply tried to list the names of those murdered but the enormity of the task forced him to give up. This experience, however, along with his discovery of the circumstances of his own mother's death in the massacre of some 12000 Jews which took place in Berdichev on 14 September 1941 sowed in his heart the seeds of *Life and Fate*: a book which is all about the need to remember.

---

[2] J & C Garrard, op. cit.170

'It seems to me,' wrote Grossman, 'that in the cruel and terrible time in which our generation has been condemned to live on this earth, we must never make peace with evil. We must never become indifferent to others or undemanding of ourselves.'[3]

For Grossman, therefore, the written word was not only a means of accessing the truth: it was also a way of keeping faith with the dead and somehow restoring them to life. This is reflected in his work between 1943 and 1946 along with Ilya Ehrenberg and the Jewish Anti-Fascist Committee on what became known as *The Black Book*, a documentary account of the massacre of Jews on Soviet and Polish soil. In a letter to Ehrenberg about *The Black Book*, Grossman said that he felt it was his moral duty to speak on behalf of the dead: 'on behalf of those who lie in the earth.' Together with his harrowing study of *The Hell of Treblinka* (1944) which was to provide invaluable evidence at the Nuremburg War Crimes trials, *The Black Book* (1993) is the most comprehensive account of the 'Shoah'.

From January 1944 onwards, therefore, Grossman set himself the task of finding out what exactly had happened to the Jewish community in Berdichev and beyond. His research led him to the conclusion that

---

[3] Ibid, 171

the Jews had borne the brunt of Nazi persecution in the Ukraine and elsewhere and that in this process many Ukrainians – especially those enrolled by the Nazis in the *Polizei* – had been complicit. Neither of these conclusions, however, were acceptable to the Soviet authorities who persisted in the myth that "all" had suffered equally in the war. Together with Grossman's determination to honour the bravery of the Russian Soldier at Stalingrad and expose the short-comings of the Soviet High Command in the war, this made it very difficult for him to find a publisher for his work after the war. As a result, Grossman's first novel about Stalingrad, *For a Just Cause*, was only published in 1950 – 52 with severe limitations attached to it.

Stalin's death on 3 March 1953, however, encouraged Grossman to start work on the second part of his novel about Stalingrad which would become, in time, *Life and Fate*. Progress on this work was, of course, assisted by the Twentieth National Congress of the Communist Party in February 1956, at which Khrushchev made his celebrated attack on Stalin as the destroyer of the party and the author of dictatorship and tyranny. Encouraged by this "thaw", Grossman worked steadily on *Life and Fate* in the 1950's and the novel was finally completed in 1960.

Unfortunately, the novel's central conclusion: that the Nazi and Soviet regimes were the mirror image of each other; that both based their appeal on nationalist extremism, and that both treated the Jews as the cause of all social and political ills, made *Life and Fate* totally unacceptable to the Soviet authorities, the "thaw" notwithstanding.[4]

Following Grossman's completion of the novel early in 1960, therefore, the authorities moved in to suppress its publication. In February 1961, the KGB arrived at Grossman's apartment to "arrest" all three manuscript copies of *Life and Fate* (two other copies, however, survived in the hands of friends). In this way the book was virtually "imprisoned".

In what remained of his life, 1960 – 64, Grossman did all he could to "free" his book, most notably in February 1962 in a moving letter to Khrushchev in which he declared:

'My book is not political…This book is as dear to me as honest children are to a father. Taking my book from me is just like taking a child from his father…I wrote the book out of love and pity for ordinary people, out of my belief in them. I ask you to release my book.'[5]

---

[4] J. C. Garrard, op. cit. 236 – 7
[5] J. C. Garrard, op. cit. 354 – 357

Grossman received no reply from Khrushchev and sadly he never lived to see the freeing of his book, and his death on 14 September 1964 - on the anniversary of his own mother's death in Berdichev - might have been the end of the story. Fortunately, through the loyalty of two of his friends (Semyon Lipkin and Lyolya Dominikina), two copies of the original manuscript had survived, and in 1974 Lipkin, with the help of Andrei Sakharov, managed to microfilm the manuscript and transfer it to the West.

Remarkably, it failed to find a publisher in the West until 1980 when a Swiss publishing house published *Life and Fate* in Russian. It was quickly translated into French and German and created a sensation. Through *glasnost* and the liberalism of the Gorbachev era the book enjoyed a "resurrection". It was finally published in Russia in 1988 and could be said to have played a significant part in the events of 1989 which led to the collapse of the Soviet empire.

Life and Fate, therefore, created quite a stir when it became available in Russia but significantly much of its central message remained unrecognised by people or politicians. This is most obviously reflected in the abiding reluctance of the Ukraine in general, and Berdichev in particular, to acknowledge their complicity in the Holocaust; or for Russia to admit the failings of Communism in terms of Stalin's anti-Semitism and his mismanagement of the War effort at the expense of soldier and civilian alike.

Grossman, therefore, remains largely unrecognised in his own country – reflected in the anonymity of his gravestone and the lack of recognition given to him in the War Memorial to Soviet Soldiers in Volgograd (Stalingrad).

His true memorial, therefore, remains his book, *Life and Fate*, which keeps alive the memory of his mother and the countless thousands sacrificed in the names of Nazism and Communism.

Please read it.

THE NOVEL

'*My book is not political. To the best of my abilities I wrote about ordinary human beings, and about their pain, their joy, their mistakes, and their deaths. I wrote of my love for human beings and of my sympathy for their suffering.*'

Vasily Grossman in a letter to Khrushchev in February 1962 asking him to "free" his book.

Life and Fate is a record of Russia's experience of the Second World War and a vivid portrait of Stalinist Russia. Its time frame centres on the crucial hundred days of street fighting from September to 18 November 1942 between the Stalingrad garrison under General Chuikov and the German Sixth Army under von Paulus. Vastly outnumbered and outgunned, the Red Army held on in Stalingrad through sheer determination and bravery until finally relieved by Zhukov's counter-offensive of 19 November 1942: the first step towards the encirclement and surrender of the German Sixth Army in February 1943.

As a war correspondent with the Red Army in Stalingrad at the time Grossman records the achievement of the Russian soldier with pride and honesty but this remains only one event in the sprawling canvas which is *Life and Fate*. It opens out to describe events happening simultaneously in the Nazi death camps in Poland and throughout the vast empire of Stalin's Soviet Union from Occupied Ukraine, to Moscow and Kuibyshev, all the way to the Far East and the camps of the Gulag. Against this background a host of different characters play out their different roles, chief among them being the Shaposhnikova family, one of whose daughters is married to Victor Shtrum, the main protagonist of the novel and Grossman's alter ego.

Emerging from this vast narrative of human interaction are Grossman's deeply-held views on the role of kindness and the individual in human affairs and the threat posed to them by totalitarian evil. It is to a consideration of these issues that I would now like to turn.

KINDNESS, THE INDIVIDUAL AND HUMANITY

'In the sight of God, all men are

One man, and one man is all men.'

Dame Julian of Norwich, *Revelations of Divine Love*

'The human experience is personal, private

And in every sense unique. That which

Each man knows he alone knows, however

Nearly like the next man's knowing

It may be. It is his, and it remains

His all through his life, right up

To the last minute of it.'

W. Saroyan, *Days of Life and Death and Escape to the Moon*

'I believe in human kindness.'

V. Grossman, *Life and Fate*

Kindness

Writing against the background of one of the darkest periods in human history, Vasily Grossman found hope in one of the most mundane of human activities, that of kindness. In a world dominated by power politics, war and ideology such an everyday virtue would seem to be powerless and it is significant that the paramountcy of kindness in *Life and Fate* is defended most passionately by the "holy fool", Ikonnikov.

Ikonnikov-Morzh is an inmate of a German concentration camp, a strange man who could have been any age at all. Fellow Russians in the camp, especially a former leading Bolshevik called Mostovskoy, look on him as a "Holy Fool" and treat him with a mixture of disgust and pity.[6]

As a young man Ikonnikov had followed the teachings of Tolstoy and became a people's teacher in a remote Russian village. After the Bolshevik Revolution he had joined a peasant commune in the hope that communist agricultural policy would achieve a heaven on earth. This hope, however, was destroyed by Stalin's policy of collectivisation and Ikonnikov himself had witnessed all the horrific

---

[6] V. Grossman (2011) 'Life and Fate', Vintage, p.10

outcome of this programme. In one vivid scene he recalls confronting an emaciated peasant, who, mad with hunger, had just eaten her children.[7]

The effect of such experience was compounded when, in June 1941, German forces invaded Byelorussia where Ikonnikov had gone to live with an older brother. There he witnessed the torments undergone by prisoners of war and the widespread persecution of the Jews. In conversation with Mostovskoy, Ikonnikov explains how this experience had come to shape his philosophy of life:

'I saw the sufferings of the peasantry with my own eyes – and yet collectivisation was carried out in the name of Good. I don't believe in your 'Good'. I believe in human kindness.'[8]

Ikonnikov later develops this theory more fully in a paper which eventually falls into the hands of Liss, the S.S. Camp administrator who dismisses it as 'rubbish', a view echoed by Mostovskoy who calls it 'trash'.

According to Ikonnikov, throughout history the idea of the 'Good' has been appropriated by religious and secular authority to justify all kinds of inhuman acts.

---

[7] V. Grossman, op. cit. 13
[8] V. Grossman, op. cit. 13

The most recent examples of this are provided by Communism and Nazism. Thus, Ikonnikov claims to have seen people in Russia during the collectivisation programme of the 1930's being slaughtered 'in the name of an idea of good as fine and humane as the ideal of Christianity.'[9]   And now, against the background of the gas chamber, Nazi fascism was doing the same thing in the name of good.

Ikonnikov, however, claims that there is an alternative to this terrible pursuit of Good with a capital 'G' and that it is to be found in everyday kindness: 'The kindness of an old woman carrying a piece of bread to a prisoner….the private kindness of one individual towards another.'[10]

According to Ikonnikov it is this petty, thoughtless kindness which is mankind's most distinctive characteristic. It can never be conquered and evil is powerless before it. This leads Ikonnikov to conclude that human history is a battle 'fought by a great evil struggling to overcome a small kernel of human kindness'[11] and one from which kindness will always emerge victorious.

---

[9] V. Grossman, op. cit. 390
[10] V. Grossman, op. cit. 391
[11] V. Grossman, op. cit. 394

Ikonnikov claims to have found evidence of such kindness even at the door of the gas chamber, and nowhere in *Life and Fate* is the power of such kindness so vividly recorded as in the relationship between Sofya Levinton and the motherless child, David.

Sofya is a Jewish army doctor captured by the Germans at Stalingrad. On the train taking her to the gas chamber she befriends a six-year old boy called David. As she reaches her destination she is conscious of a deep sense of isolation: the inability ever to communicate the secret of one's soul: 'You carry away this sense of your life without ever having shared it with anyone.'[12]

Alongside this consciousness of an individual life, however, is a growing affection and sense of responsibility for David which overcomes Sofya's instinct for survival and sees her remain silent when the Nazi guards call for any doctors and surgeons to make themselves known.

Her self-sacrifice at this point is the product of her growing tenderness towards David, for whom she now feels as a mother for her child: 'Eat my son, eat,' she says as she offers him some bread. And so, Sofya

---

[12] V. Grossman, op. cit. 527

and David enter the gas chamber together, mother and child. 'Sofya Levinton felt the boy's body subside in her arms.... This boy with his slight, bird-like body had left before her. 'I've become a mother,' she thought. That was her last thought.'[13] Her senseless kindness had brought its reward.

---

[13] V. Grossman, op. cit. 538

The Individual

Growing out of Grossman's theory of kindness and supportive of it is his belief in the paramount importance of the individual. This, of course, is somewhat surprising given that Grossman had spent so much of his working life in the service of a political philosophy in which the individual is definitely subordinate to the State. His experience of Stalinist oppression in the 1930's, however, caused him to begin to question the basis of this philosophy and his experience as a war correspondent with the Red Army in Stalingrad and as a witness to the Holocaust led him, in *Life and Fate*, to champion the paramountcy of the individual in human affairs.

Given Grossman's admiration for the bravery and the fortitude displayed by so many individual Russian soldiers in the battle for Stalingrad it is perhaps appropriate that the most articulate defence of the role of the individual in *Life and Fate* is provided by a military man, Colonel Pyotr Novikov, commanding officer of a Tank Corps at Stalingrad.

On the night before the offensive which would bring an end to the siege, Novikov, observing the growing mass of men and materials before him, reflects upon the huge diversity of human life displayed: a soldier singing; another thinking about home; one trying to identify a bird on a tree.[14] For Novikov these may be trivial thoughts but, nonetheless, thoughts which give meaning to life. This leads him to conclude, along with Grossman, that human society is, in fact, all about such trivialities and exists only in order to preserve them; that the State and Religion have no right to determine what our priorities should be; and that 'the only true and lasting meaning of the struggle for life lies in the individual, in his modest peculiarities, and in his right to these peculiarities.'[15]

There is no clearer statement of Vasily Grossman's philosophy of life.

---

[14] V. Grossman, op. cit. 212-13

[15] V. Grossman op. cit. 214

Humanity

Humanity is another theme addressed by Grossman in *Life and Fate* and it is intimately associated with his philosophy of kindness and the individual. Chekhov is his inspiration here and it is "his" theory of humanity which is defended by the historian, Leonid Madyarov, in conversation with Victor Shtrum.

According to Madyarov Chekhov had insisted on the primacy of humanity in our evaluation of each other. Social, political, economic, religious or ethnic differences do not define us or determine our value in society. As human beings we are all equal and as individuals we all have a right to be respected.

'Chekhov said:...Let's begin with respect, compassion and love for the individual – or we'll never get anywhere. That's democracy, the still unrealised democracy of the Russian people.'[16]

---

[16] V. Grossman, op. cit. 267

LIFE AS A BOOK

'The Book of Life is brief

And once a page is read

All but Love is dead

That is my belief.'

Don McLean, "And I love you so"

Amid all the frustration surrounding the "imprisonment" of his work Grossman found consolation and inspiration in his belief in the power of the written word to bring to life the otherwise forgotten dead. This is most perfectly expressed in a letter which Grossman wrote in 1961 to his mother – as if she were still alive – on the twentieth anniversary of her death on 14 September 1941. The same letter, of course, reflects Grossman's sense of guilt over his failure to get his mother out of Berdichev before the Germans arrived in July 1941.

'Dear Mama. It is now twenty years since your death. I love you; I remember you every day of my life, and the pain of your loss has stayed with me constantly over these past twenty years. Ten years ago when I wrote you my first letter after your death, you remained just the same as when you were alive, my mother in my body and my soul. I am you, dear Mama, and as long as I live, then you are alive also. When I die you will continue to live in this book - Life and Fate – which I have dedicated to you and whose fate is closely tied with your fate....'[17]

Grossman's concept of a book as being a living thing is perhaps echoed in the following observations by

---

[17] J. & C. Garrard, op. cit. 353

John Donne in a meditation on death that he wrote in 1623:

'All mankind is of one author, and is one volume. When one man dies one chapter is not torne out of the book, but translated into a better language; and every chapter must be so translated. God employs several translators: some pieces are translated by age, some by sickness, some by war, some by justice; but God's hand is in every translation and his hand shall bind up all our scattered leaves, for that library where every book shall lie open to one another.' Devotio XVII

From this point of view every life is a book and the sum-total forms a library of human experience. At the same time it is a commonplace that the world is a stage on which we each play out our different roles. It follows that each life is a play in which a cast of many, or a few, act out their parts and engage with the central character – me or you.

I suppose that all literature is simply a record of this inter-action; but inevitably this record is highly selective so that the vast majority of us go "unwritten-up."

In an attempt to make some very partial amends for this over-sight we should perhaps simply record the names of all those who form the cast of our lives, either directly through their personal contact with us, or indirectly through their public works. Such a *Dramatis Personae* might serve to express what we meant to each other and what our play was all about.[18]

I think Vasily Grossman would have liked that.

[18] D. Conduct (2017) The Holy Contour of Life, Publish Nation, p.12

'The human race is a family;

Not a competition.'

D. Conduct, *The Holy Contour of Life*, p. 17

The paradox of our human condition is that we are all both uniquely individual and at the same time all dependent on each other. We are not alone. The human race is a family, not a competition and our self-fulfilment depends upon our recognition of this fact.

We do not exist as separate individuals but as members of a family and this means both celebrating our individuality and recognising the common humanity that we all share. It means rejoicing in the success of others and finding comfort in their joy. It also means grieving at their failure and their loss, for every person's private sorrow is a public grief and every funeral bell rings for us all.

'No man is an island,' wrote the Seventeenth Century divine, John Donne, 'entire of itself. Every man is a piece of the Continent; part of the Main; if a clod be washed away by the sea Europe is the less as well as if a Promontory were. Any man's death diminishes me, because I am involved in mankind. And therefore never send to know for whom the bell tolls. It tolls for thee.'[19]

But, let Vasily have the final word: the happiness of human life springs only from the existence of

---

[19] J. Donne 'Devotio XVII'

someone *'as a whole world that has never been repeated in all eternity.'* [20]

[20] V. Grossman *Life and Fate*, 539